Life: Life Is For Everyone

Joanna White

Published by Joanna White, 2022.

Table of Contents

To my family, for always supporting me. To all of the mothers and fathers who have difficulty having kids - you are not alone. To all of the mothers and fathers who have chosen to get an abortion in the past - God can forgive you and you can heal. To every single child that has been murdered in the womb. Lastly, to God, for all that He has done.

Life: Life Is For Everyone

Copyright © 2022 by Joanna White

First edition June 2022

Introduction

What defines a human? Is it our eye color or hair? Is it our personalities, our hobbies, what we like or dislike? Is it our voices or senses? Or is it more technical—our brains and nerves? Is it our hearts that beat and keep us alive?

People who are for abortion oftentimes focus on the mother. It's her body, so it's her choice. She has rights too, and so on. What they forget is that there is another human life inside her now, so it isn't just her body anymore.

"No, that is just a fetus," one would argue. Abortion doctors and anyone who is pro-abortion will say the same thing. It's just a fetus. If you look at any abortion clinic website or even blog posts asking about how the abortion will go, they use terms like "terminate pregnancy" and "remove pregnancy tissue." It's a "fetus."

What do these terms do?

They dehumanize.

They use these terms because, then, it's a fetus, not a baby. If it's a fetus, then it isn't murder. That's the same thing that people did to African American people during the times of slavery. The derogatory terms used against them was used to dehumanize all African Americans—so that they were seen as slaves and beasts, beneath whites in society. The same thing happened to Native Americans—they were called savages... why?

To dehumanize them.

What we are doing to *babies* is no different.

So, I ask again: what defines a human? Not the color of our skin, as we know already. Racism plays a huge role in society—people who feel we still have it, people who want to stop it, and others who don't think or dwell on it too much. Not our sexuality, because we are told that a man can be a woman and a woman can be a man.

When society uses terms and starts to dehumanize any type of person, it's used as a justification for harming them. We've seen this time and time again throughout history. It doesn't matter whether the term is: nigger, savage, or fetus, the goal is to dehumanize and destroy.

Life Inside the Womb

You are still inside your mother's womb. At 3 weeks, your heart starts to beat. This means that at 21 days old, before your mother even knows she's pregnant with you, your heart is already alive and beating. A few days after that is when your mother will likely learn about your existence.

During week 5, your hands and wrist joints begin to form. One day, those same wrists and hands may play an instrument—like the piano or guitar. They may one day write a best-selling book, or even hold a child of your own. But for now, they are slowly developing, aided by the forming of your limbs and the cranial nerves. At this stage, you're already moving, even though your mother can't quite feel the movements yet.

By the next week, the bones inside your arms and legs have formed and your brain activity is starting. You have eye lids and a primitive nasal cavity as well. You're already starting to develop some of your vital organs: kidneys, liver, pancreas, lungs, stomach, and intestines.

Week 7 is when you are finally able to hiccup for the first time. Your head can rotate and your legs move. You've also just learned how to touch your hands to each other and even overlap your fingers. Your heart is fully formed at this stage and your toes and knee joints are finally starting to develop.

But wait, the very next week, the hair on your eyebrows and mouth have formed. Your eyelids are finally fused together and your joints are similar to that of an adult. By week 9, you can suck your thumb, yawn, and your vocal cords have formed. At week 10, your fingernails and toenails begin to grow and you already have your unique fingerprints that identifies you from every other human being on the planet. Your bones solidify during this week as well, and you can roll your eyes.

Just a week later, at week 11, with your nose and lips fully formed, you can make facial expressions. Your gender and reproductive organs have formed and your weight will increase at over 60% during this time. A week after that, you have taste buds, your bowel movements begin, and your hands touch your mouth on average of 50 times in a single hour.

Week 13, your teeth are growing and your kidneys have fully formed. By this time, your body is already sensitive to touch. A week after that, your cerebral cortex has four lobes, just like an adult.

3 weeks later, your mother can finally feel your movements. Your teeth enamel is starting to form, and your body has fully developed hormonal stress that happens as a result of invasive procedures. By the time week 18 happens, your eyes and ears are in their final position, and the bones in your ear and the nerves in your brain allow you to be able to pick up sounds. You also have sweat glands and insulin.

Just a week later, if you're a female, your oogonia have formed and will one day become eggs so that you too may one day have a baby of your own. If you're a male, your prostate gland starts to form. Your life has already developed a steady schedule every day, such as sleeping.

At week 20, your skin layers and structures are fully developed. The cochlea inside your inner ear is actually the same size as an adult's, is fully formed, and you can respond to sounds you hear from outside the womb. You can open your eyes and your head is about 20 centimeters in circumference. Just a week later, your legs are at their correct proportions, hair grows on your scalp, and your brain has developed the same way it will be all the way until you are five years old. At this stage of your development, if you are born prematurely, you have a 50% chance of surviving.

At 23 weeks, your white blood cells help you fight off infections, hearing is as clear as it ever will be, your brain will increase in size at around 400%, and your nostrils open. During this time, you're busy moving around to help develop your body's muscles.

Within the next two weeks, you can fully hear outside the womb to the point where loud, sudden noises will startle you, and increase your heart rate and movement. Your eyes can now see light and color, and you have fully developed your sense of taste. If your mother eats something sweet, for example, you will swallow faster, but you'll swallow bitter foods slower. The lining in your intestines have the exact same cell types that you will have as an adult.

Two weeks after this, during weeks 26 and 27, you will fully develop your sense of smell, you may fully develop your ability to form tears, your eyelashes are growing, your pupils will react to light, and you can regulate your body temperature after you're born.

During week 28, you can tell the difference between high-pitched sounds and low-pitched sounds outside your mother's womb. You can do summersaults with a series of movements that are similar to walking. In the week following, your head is proportional to your body now, you have all five of your senses, your eyes can move, and space is becoming limited inside your mother's womb, so you can't move as easily.

By week 31, your body practices the act of breathing, even though there isn't any air inside your mother's womb. You will also have dreams. During week 32, your memory will start to work, and you will prefer songs that you listened to while your mother was pregnant with you over ones played only after you were born. Your lower esophagus muscles are fully functional at this stage as well.

At 35 weeks, you can now grip things and you will be gaining about half a pound every week. Your lungs have fully developed and are ready to help you breathe outside the womb.

When week 39 hits, everything inside you is ready to give birth at any time. You have well over 300 bones in your body.

The baby will be capable of crying at birth, though tears may not appear because of underdeveloped tear ducts.

What Abortion Really Is

There are different types of abortion procedures given to women at different stages of pregnancy. The first is through abortion pills. During the first several weeks (up to 10 weeks) of a pregnancy, the mother makes an appointment at an abortion clinic and she's given a pill that has Mifepristone (also called RU-486). What this drug does is that it blocks an important and vital hormone called progesterone. This hormone is naturally produced inside the mother's body to help nourish your baby and sustain the child throughout the pregnancy. What Mifepristone does is that it blocks progesterone. When this happens, the lining of the mother's uterus breaks down, which completely blocks blood and nourishment to the baby. As a result, the baby will die.

It starves the baby to death.

Babies at this stage in the pregnancy already have wrist and hand joints. He or she can move their head and legs, and they can hiccup. The baby has vocal cords, can suck their thumb, and even yawn! More importantly, *the baby already has a heartbeat.*

Once the baby is dead, the mother is given Misoprostol (also called Cytotec) which causes the mother's body to expel the baby.

The second type of abortion that's done is called aspiration abortion, also called D&C which means dilation and curettage.

With this type of abortion procedure, the mother will have a few visits to the clinic for ultrasounds and to examine the state of her pregnancy. After that, the abortion doctor will use metal rods to dilate the mother's cervix, that way, the doctor is able to reach the baby.

The abortion doctor takes a suction catheter that is 10 to 20 times stronger than a household vacuum cleaner to suck the baby out of the womb. Once the child has been removed, the abortion doctor will use a device called a curette, which is a sharp metal object, to scrape the lining of the uterus and remove any remaining parts of the baby. This is done anywhere between five and thirteen weeks of pregnancy—when the baby has eyebrows and can make facial expressions, including rolling the baby's eyes, and can also taste things.

This is when the baby can feel pain and is sensitive to touch.

Another abortion procedure is called induction abortion. It takes several days to complete the procedure. At day 1, the abortion doctor will inject the baby with digoxin or potassium chloride to ensure that the baby goes into cardiac arrest and dies. At this point, the abortion doctor will also use laminaria sticks (or sterilized seaweed) to open up the mother's cervix. On day 2, the abortion doctor will replace the laminaria and check to see if the baby is dead or alive. If the baby still lives, the abortion doctor will inject it with a secondary lethal dose of digoxin or potassium chloride. The mother will have to wait a few days for her cervix to completely dilate so she can deliver the baby. The baby will be delivered dead—after being given a heart attack.

This is done from 25 weeks pregnant all the way up until birth. At this stage, the baby can hear sounds outside the womb and can distinguish the difference between high-pitched and low-pitched sounds. The baby tastes what the mother eats, and loud sounds will startle the child. The baby has hair, can move, and their body is fully developed as they gain weight.

This is when the baby can do summersaults in the womb.

The final abortion procedure that's done is the most gruesome, which is why I waited until last to explain it. It's called a D&E, or a dilatation and evacuation abortion. The abortion doctor will once again use laminaria to open the mother's cervix anywhere from one to two days before the procedure. During the procedure itself, the abortion doctor may put the mother under anesthesia. Then, the abortion doctor will insert a large suction catheter into the uterus, which will empty the womb of amniotic fluid. As soon as the fluid is all gone, the abortion doctor grabs a tool that's called a sopher clamp. This tool is a device used for grasping that has rows of sharp teeth on the clamps. This is used to grasp the baby's legs and arms and tear them from the baby's body. The abortion doctor uses this tool to grasp the baby's intestines, spine, heart, lungs, arms, legs, and any other parts of the body to rip the baby's body into pieces small enough to fit outside the womb. The hardest part of the procedure comes when the abortion doctor must locate the baby's head, grasp it, and crush it. Meticulously, the abortion doctor will remove pieces of the baby's skull, and then use a curette to scrape the uterus and remove the placenta and any parts of the baby remaining.

The abortion doctor has to reassemble the baby's body to ensure all the pieces are there. This torturous, sadistic procedure happens from 13 to 24 weeks. This is after the baby already has skin, hair, can hear and live outside the womb...

And after the baby can feel pain.

In medieval times, once of the worst ways of execution was called drawing and quartering. A human who was going to be executed would have his or her limbs tied to four horses who would then be spurred to take off running. The force of the horses running would rip the limbs from the victim off their torso and kill them.

This is what we are doing to infant children—defenseless babies who don't have a voice, can't stand up for themselves. We are having them drawn and quartered.

Infant babies.

The Holocaust

According to history.com, the holocaust refers to the "ideological and systematic state-sponsored persecution and mass murder of millions of European Jews (as well as millions of others, including Romani people, the intellectually disabled, dissidents, and homosexuals) by the German Nazi regime between 1933 and 1945," (History Editors, 2021). Adolf Hitler believed that Germans were the number one race in the world. He firmly believed that Jews were inferior as a race, and were a threat to Germans being pure.

It all started with simple things, such as requirements for them to be identified publicly, and resulted in years of them being persecuted leading up to the Holocaust. Hitler had concentration camps built in Poland, which were execution centers. Around six million Jews and 5 million other people died during the Holocaust, including homosexuals and the disabled.

Auschwitz was one of the most infamous death camps, where over 2 million people were murdered. Both Jews and non-Jews worked there. Jewish people were gassed and thousands more died from starvation and disease. Then, in the year 1943, Josef Mengele started experimenting on innocent people, specifically twins, which is why he became known as "the Angel of Death."

The world has spent the years afterward recovering, not just from the effects of World War II, but of the Holocaust itself. The Jews have suffered enormously since then, including riots, racism, and persecution that took place at the hands of Europeans even after the war was over. They became refugees and had to travel to other countries, some of which still had strict immigration laws. The United States lifted their restrictions and over 68,000 Jews immigrated to America. As a result of all this, the State of Israel was formed in the year 1948 and over 170,000 Jews migrated there by 1953.

6 million Jews mass murdered and 5 million other people on top of that. Over 11 million people were murdered during the Holocaust and countless others were killed from the war itself. What Hitler did has widely been considered genocide because of the staggering number of innocent people killed.

Now, let me give you some other numbers that may shock you as much as it shocked me.

36,707,730 abortions have taken place worldwide and that number goes up by one every second. If you visit the website worldometers, you can watch as the number continues to rise. This is equal to 125,000 abortions per day worldwide and over 3,000 of those are just in the US alone. For the United States, 22% of all pregnancies end in abortion, and that isn't including miscarriages.

22%! That's one fifth of all pregnancies in the US! So, one out of every five women in America have abortions!

If 11 million deaths of people is still considered genocide (as it should be), then why are we ignoring this new holocaust that has found its way into the world today? The worst part of all this is that at least people acknowledge that Hitler was wrong, and that what happened to countless Jews and people back in the 1940s was wrong. Today, people all over the world, especially here in the United States, think that abortion is okay. In 2018, only 28% of women would vote to overturn the Roe Vs. Wade decision: 14% of female democrats and 49% of female republicans.

In 2021, 49% of all Americans are pro-abortion, which leaves 47% who are pro-life, and only 2% are neutral.

If a man murdered a pregnant woman, would he be convicted of a single or double homicide? If you say double, then why is abortion not murder? If you say single, then why does the baby's life not count as a life?

Here is a fact that all pro-abortionists ignore, one crucial piece of simple, scientific logic that they ignore: *babies are human.* They aren't just a "fetus" as I mentioned earlier. That term and other scientific ones have been used to dehumanize the babies and to desensitize us as people to what abortion really is at its heart: murder.

When Black Lives Matter groups rioted in 2020, it created a huge controversy in the United States. They rallied to a cause they believed needed to be addressed because Black Lives Matter. Many people felt that black lives were being targeted and killed deliberately and that this had become a major problem that needed to be addressed across the country, sometimes even violently so.

There were 123 total reported black people shot by police in 2020. There were 80 Hispanics shot by police in 2020. Out of these, 2.8 times more black people died from their gunshot wounds versus the white people. And in 2021, that number has dropped down to 111. There is also 340 people who were shot to death by police whose race is unknown. Any death is a terrible and tragic loss and my heart goes out to anyone who is shot and killed, especially innocent people who don't deserve it. Every single innocent African American who has been shot and killed is tragic, just like the 11 million innocent people murdered by Hitler is tragic.

Just like the 36 million babies murdered all around the world.

At least African Americans have a voice. At least the Jews and other people coming out of the horrors of the Holocaust had a voice. They have adults...men, women, old, and young, people who not only were old enough to speak for themselves, but to shout out and say something, to bring the world's attention to the injustices that happened against them

But those 36 million infants in the womb being aborted?

They're in the womb. They're growing. Maturing. At 3 weeks, they have heartbeats. They can't speak yet. They have no voice. No one to speak for them, to defend them. To cry out for justice for them.

They're told that they aren't human; that it's the woman's choice. Their choices are ripped away from them.

Pro-abortion isn't pro-choice; it's stripping away the lives of innocent people who have no voice at all. It's no different than what Hitler did when he dehumanized the Jews and murdered them.

11 million people is enough to outrage the world and affect it for years after the Holocaust. It's enough to teach people that all races matter, to take measures to prevent horrors like this from ever happening again.

Yet 36 million babies are murdered and it's considered a procedure. A woman's choice. It isn't just her body, and it isn't just her choice. The baby has a right to live.

"A nation that kills its children in the womb has lost its soul." - Mother Teresa

Reasons for Abortion

What about a woman's choice? I'm a woman and I'm all for women's rights and choices and freedoms. I love that we can vote and have more rights than ever before, like owning businesses and making a name for ourselves. But when it comes to abortion, it isn't just the woman's life here. What about the life of the unborn child? That baby will one day grow up and become an adult—they will love and work and play and grow, just like their mother did. They have a right to life and a right to have the choice to live.

But what about the woman's choice to have an abortion? Here are some of the most common reasons given, and this is based on a study called the *Turnaway Study*.

1) The woman isn't financially prepared.

This can range from anything to financial problems, being unemployed, can't get insurance, welfare, or food stamps, and even don't want government assistance. I can't speak for what it's like to be homeless. All I know are my own life experiences. My parents were divorced and my mother was a single mother raising two kids. At one point, she was unemployed and all we had was a small child support check and some food stamps. There were times we didn't know where our next meal would come from. What got us through was trusting in God and He took care of us. The Bible says not to worry about food or drink, and that if God cares for the birds and the lilies, how much more will He care for us?

Now, I know not everyone believes in God, and even sometimes, those who do, don't trust Him to provide. That aside, this isn't a good enough reason for an abortion. Firstly, plenty of people who have started off dirt poor and homeless have went on to live successful lives, including J-Lo who became homeless after she left home at 18, Steve Jobs after he dropped out of college, Silvester Stallone before he made the *Rocky* movies even had to sell his dog for $50, and more like Halle Berry, Chris Pratt, Jim Carrey, and even Dr. Phil.

Should we kill all poor people then?

I would hope that your answer to that question is no. If not, seek psychiatric care. Think about all the poor people in third world countries. They have a right to live just like we do.

Secondly, do I think that we need to offer more financial aide, both to women who are pregnant and for health care in general? Yes. We absolutely should. Help out third world countries and kids starving in Africa, which is heartbreaking. But care for them. Provide for them.

Don't murder them.

2) The woman says it isn't the right time for the baby.

This ranges from the pregnancy being unplanned and she isn't prepared to be a mother, to the woman either being too young or too old to have a child. Firstly, many unplanned pregnancies happen all the time. But even with contraceptives out there, sex is never an act without consequences.

The best contraceptive is abstinence!

If you aren't ready to have a child, then you shouldn't be having sex! Just like if you can't handle alcohol very well, then you shouldn't be drinking. This is why we have an age limit on when you can drink, because anyone under 21 isn't legally considered being able to handle the consequences of drinking.

Yes, as humans, we all crave and want sex. This is why God designed it to be within the boundary of marriage! Sex is meant to be a beautiful thing, when it is used as God intended. That is why God intended for it to be something that takes place between one man and one woman who are married; in being married, there is a mother and a father who are both there to help provide for the child.

3) The woman's partner

This ranges from the relationship being bad or new, to her wanting to be married before she has a child, to that she doesn't love her partner, or that he isn't supportive, is abusive, or doesn't want the baby.

This is definitely not a good reason to murder a child. Should we murder all children who come from divorce? As a child whose parents were divorced, I hope you don't believe that. Plenty of fathers don't want their children. Plenty of mothers don't want their children either. That isn't the point and it certainly isn't a justification for murdering a child.

For a woman in an abusive situation, my heart goes out to you. I know that the woman in an abusive relationship may be terrified and I can only imagine the horror that she's going through. There are a lot of places that are there to help women in abusive households. You can get away and be free! Even if you have no help, seek it!

Don't murder a child for the sins of the father.

My father abandoned my mother, sister, and I, but that didn't mean she murdered us. It meant life was harder for all of us, but no one ever said life was going to be easy. Life will never be easy; so, murdering a baby to try to make life easier isn't going to work. Somewhere down your life, you'll encounter something else that's hard—another struggle, another difficulty. Life will never be easier for you. The sooner you accept that, then the more readily you can face the difficulties to come.

4) The woman needs to focus on other children

This ranges from the woman having enough children right now, or got pregnant too soon after having a child already, all the way to her concern for the other children she is raising. This reflects back on whether we should murder all poor people. Does one child have the right to live over another?

More than that, there are actually a high number of children who had siblings that were aborted either after them, or sometimes with them—as in, they were the twin who survived an abortion procedure. They end up with survivor's guilt and PTSD because they were the child who survived.

5) The pregnancy interferes with her future opportunities

This ranges from a woman's educational and vocational plans, to that she wants a better life for herself. I'll touch more on this one later, but how selfish is it to say that "I want a better educational opportunity, so I'm going to murder a child." That's no different than someone who wants a promotion at work coming in and murdering the person who has the job they want, just so they can get it.

In the Bible, some of the nations that God allowed Israel to defeat were ones that practiced child sacrifice. They would take their babies and children and kill them on the alter to false gods like Baal and Dagon. We may not worship statues, but idols are anything in our lives that we put before God.

When women commit abortions for their own selfish ambitions or men pressure them to do so, it's no different than the child-sacrificing cults in ancient times.

6) The woman is not emotionally or mentally prepared

This one is pretty straightforward. What parent is, though? Every mother goes through the same fears and reservations when she's pregnant; not just being unsure whether she'll make a good mother, but feeling as if she is completely unprepared. Maybe she still has emotional growth to do, but none of us ever stop emotionally growing. Or maybe she has mental issues that she still needs to work through. Firstly, she should go get help, if financially possible. I can attest to this one, as I have issues that I need therapy for, but can't afford the help right now. This is when the woman should seek help from friends, family, and/or the father, if he's around. If she doesn't have anyone, there are lots of apps and online forums these days to help.

If we try to wait until we're prepared to have children, then we never will be. I feel for people with mental or emotional problems; I have my own as well, and I have been around others who have them too. But that is still not a justification for murdering someone. If you wouldn't murder a 3-year-old child (and I sincerely hope you don't think that's okay) because of your issues, then don't murder an innocent baby over it either.

7) The woman has a health issue

This ranges from the woman has concern for the health of the baby, or has used drugs, tobacco, alcohol, or prescription or contraceptive drugs. For now, I'm just going to address the only health issues mentioned in the study... Firstly, if a woman is concerned for the health of the baby, killing it probably isn't the best idea. "Killing is a mercy" one might argue. In certain situations, perhaps, such as a person who is in a coma who will no longer wake. That is still a debated topic and usually, doctors will first go to the person's wishes in the situation, and their family later to decide. Even then, the decision is done with great mourning at "pulling the plug" on someone who can't survive on their own. It is never a decision made lightly and is only done in situations where the person is never going to get better—never going to wake again. The difference here is that a baby is (usually, in most cases) only going to grow and continue to develop and become more mentally developed as they age. Whereas a coma patient is brain dead and, in the situations where they are taken off life support, never will again.

Yet there are many other health issues that seem agonizing and painful, but they're ones that people live with and survive through all the time. These are known as disabilities and there are countless ones all over the world. If you look up online, you can find some of the most amazing and courageous stories, ranging from a man who was bent over himself and ended up having surgery much later in life to survive, to countless other people who have survived the worst health conditions possible.

The key is that they *survived*.

People with disabilities are still people, and babies with disabilities and health problems are still people too. Thirdly, if a woman is using drugs, alcohol, tobacco, not only should they not be having sex and risking the consequence of that which is pregnancy, but that reflects back on the previous one about sacrificing an innocent child for a person's own selfish idols.

Lastly, and this one wasn't included in the study, there are some people who genuinely have a health risk when having a child. My mom had the RH-factor when she was pregnant with me. I don't know how things have improved since I was born and if it's easier now to carry a child with this condition, but when she was pregnant with me, she was told that I wouldn't survive. Now, here I am, alive and breathing. Sometimes, there are greater risks, ones that will kill either the baby eventually, or sometimes the mother and the baby. I do believe that if there is no other choice, then by ending the child's life, you are saving the mother—but only if there is no other choice. Even then, it's still a conflicting thing, as I personally think it should all be left in God's hands, but it's a horrible, tragic situation, and if both are going to die, then you would actually be saving a life. These situations should always be taken very seriously and the people involved should go to God in prayer about them.

8) The woman wants a better life for the baby than she could provide

This ranges from she wants a better life for the baby, or her housing situation isn't suitable for a baby, she doesn't have proper childcare or help from her family to care for the child, or doesn't want the child to have a childhood like hers. This reason makes no sense to me at all. If a woman wants a better life for her child, then how is murdering the baby giving him or her a better life?

Murdering the child is *robbing* the child of life!

My other question (one I've asked before) is... with this logic, then, should we just go murder every homeless person or child raised in a poor household? Whatever happen to the encouraging and inspiring success stories where dirt-poor people go on to live incredible lives and make something of themselves?

Or should we go on and murder every single child who is abused? There are countless stories of people who have been abused as a child, in the most ruthless of ways, who are alive today. Yes, they went through some of the most horrific things imaginable. And yes, at times, they probably wished that they were dead. But now, afterward, they have worked toward healing and overcoming their trauma and are alive and well—and glad to be so.

9) The woman isn't independent or mature enough to have a baby

This ranges from the woman being too young or immature to have a baby, to she can't take care of herself or is dependent on others right now. My hope is that a woman in this situation could get help from friends, family, or her partner. But even if none of those options are available to her, it doesn't justify the murder of a child. Pro-abortionists don't like to hear this one, but adoption is an option. I know the foster system is terrible, but there are countless people who have endured abuse and horrific things in their pasts and have grown up and become stronger and overcome these terrible things. Sometimes, children suffer these same horrifying abuses at the hands of their own blood family; so, it doesn't just happen to kids in the foster system. But again, that doesn't justify murder. Unless you're saying we should go murder children in the foster care system.

I do think more money needs to be given not only to the foster care system, but to help women who are pregnant so they can afford to go to the doctor. In a perfect world, everyone could go to the doctor without worrying about finances—and every child in the foster care system would be properly cared for.

10) The woman was influenced by her family or friends

This ranges from the woman's pregnancy would negatively impact her family or friends, to she didn't want her close friends or family to know and was afraid they would judge her, all the way to her friends and family pressured her to get an abortion. In this one, I really hope the woman can decide for herself what to do. Don't kill a child just because everyone else around you is urging you do. What if they were urging you to commit murder on someone else? Would you do it? I would hope the answer is a resounding no! It may be hard and the whole world may be against you, but killing that child is the worst mistake of your life. One day, that child will grow up. They'll have a name and hobbies, things that he or she likes to do, and things that they don't like to do. They'll have a favorite color and a favorite season and will yawn and suck their thumb in the womb around the time that you want to kill them.

Don't let someone else decide whether your child should live or die. Choose life! What if that were you?

I bet if you offered to kill them, they would want to live at all costs!

11) Rape

Again, this one is straightforward. Short disclaimer on this one, this reason was NOT included in the study—so none of the women in the study had rape listed as a reason, but it is a reason, just a rare one. So, I am still listing it here. Firstly, I just want to note that only 1% of women get an abortion due to rape, and only 0.5% because of incest, according to the Guttmacher Institute.

I have witnessed the effects of rape and what it can do to a person—from PTSD, to the feeling that you are dirty and guilty and unwanted, to feeling helpless and powerless and hopeless. Sometimes, anger and rage and even suicide at times. I know the horrors of rape and how terrible it is. My heart goes out to every woman who endures rape—and every man, because yes, men can and do get raped. But I beg you to hear me now:

One sin does not justify another.

Do not murder an innocent child for the sins of the father. I cannot imagine the feelings of being violated being increased a hundred times over after discovering that your rapist got you pregnant. It must be so horrifying. And in that moment, the temptation to get an abortion and get rid of all reminders of what you went through must be tempting beyond what words can fully describe. But that child does not deserve to die for what evil his or her father did against you.

What if you were the result of a rape? You live and breathe, and enjoy life (I would hope so. If you have or are contemplating suicide, please contact the National Suicide Prevention Lifeline at 800-273-8255). You have your likes and dislikes and personality quirks that make you unique. Try to imagine the things that make this baby unique.

This child is a gift—a gift from God to you, something beautiful that He wants to bring out of something so tragic and ugly. I have heard stories from women who were raped who went on to have a child as a result of the rape and now love their child deeply and are happy they had the baby.

It will be hard and difficult, but don't become a monster just because of what a monster did to you. Getting rid of this child isn't going to ease your pain or erase what happened to you. You are not alone.

Regardless of a woman's reasons for abortion (and remember that the majority of reasons for an abortion is financial or because they weren't ready or wanted a better future for themselves, and only 1% due to rape), murdering an innocent child is *never* alright.

"I've noticed that everyone who is for abortion has already been born." - Ronald Reagan

Arguments For Abortion (and responses to them)

<u>Argument 1</u>

The first argument for abortion is one that may surprise people who don't really know much about the abortion debate or don't pay attention to it. But the first argument is that Roe v. Wade claimed that abortion was a Constitutional right for women to have.

The problem with this argument is that Roe v. Wade was a decision that itself was unconstitutional, which is the reason why it deserves to be overturned. The claim was that because the Constitution grants a right to privacy in certain areas or zones, the right to privacy is broad enough to include a woman's decision to have an abortion.

By ruling this, Roe v. Wade essentially took the power of deciding about abortion away from the states, which meant it wasn't voted on by the people. No one got to vote on this and choose whether we wanted abortion legal or illegal, or whether there needed to be any restrictions on it.

Thus, overturning Roe v. Wade only grants this power to decide about abortion back to the states—people will vote on the issue in each individual state. So, liberal states who are for it will keep it legal, and conservative states won't. That's where the power should lie—for the people to decide on this issue and vote to make a decision. Especially about an issue so serious and controversial.

This argument that a woman's right to have an abortion is Constitutional is a lie. Firstly, abortion was never something mentioned in the original Constitution. Second, the Constitution states the opposite. Amendment 8 of the Bill of Rights says, "Excessive bail shall not be required, nor excessive fines imposed, nor cruel and unusual punishments inflicted."

Bail and fines are referring to people in prison, but if it's illegal for criminals in prison to not be treated with cruel and unusual punishments, then why wouldn't that apply to all human beings? Torturing people is illegal as well—that's a serious crime.

As we've talked about in this book already, the methods used to kill an unborn baby is certainly cruel and unusual.

<u>Argument 2</u>

The second argument for abortion is that a woman has a right to be independent and to choose her own future—including having control over reproduction.

No one would argue that everyone shouldn't have a right to what happens to their own bodies, or that women shouldn't decide whether to have children or not. But there are several issues with this particular argument where it pertains to abortion.

Firstly, in most cases of abortion, the woman chose to have sex and knew the consequences of doing that action—sex generally leads to pregnancy, so having a child is a consequence of that action. What sex is biologically designed to do is to have a child. Thus, she made the choice and should face the consequences of that choice. You don't get to kill someone just because you made a mistake and got pregnant. If you weren't ready to have a child—emotionally, financially, or otherwise—then you shouldn't have been having sex. It's harsh but plain, simple, and true.

Secondly, the right to your body is a right, yes, but it isn't just your body anymore. There is a completely separate, new, living human being inside a mother's womb—and it isn't just a leach or something sucking the life out of the mother. It's a baby, one that will grow and only continue to grow and become more developed and active with life.

You could try to argue that a woman's womb is still part of her body, and, thus, she has the right to do whatever she wants with it. But to that I would argue that a uterus is a very unique organ—whereas every other organ in our bodies is designed to help us and make our lives better, a uterus is specifically designed to carry another human being and help it survive.

Thirdly, a parent has a moral obligation to care for their children. It's why if you were to starve an infant days after it was born, you would be arrested and charged with neglect—while, on the other hand, no one is charged with neglect if they choose not to donate to help starving children around the world. It's a parent's moral obligation to care for their children.

Finally, to close this argument, while a woman has a right to her own body, *every* human does. What about the baby's right? If women's rights are so important, what about the little child in the womb and his or her right to live?

<u>Argument 3</u>

The third argument for abortion is not scientifically or biologically accurate. This argument claims that a baby isn't alive until the child is able to survive outside the womb—to people who use this argument, that is when personhood begins. Along with this, people who use this argument point out that our age is counted from the moment of birth and that babies are not independent, self-determining beings, so abortion is just terminating a pregnancy, not killing a human being.

The fact that life begins at conception is not just a religious belief, it's science—a simple, biological fact.

"Development of the embryo begins at Stage 1 when a sperm fertilizes an oocyte and together they form a zygote." [England, Marjorie A. Life Before Birth. 2nd ed. England: Mosby-Wolfe, 1996, p.31]

"Human development begins after the union of male and female gametes or germ cells during a process known as fertilization (conception). Fertilization is a sequence of events that begins with the contact of a sperm (spermatozoon) with a secondary oocyte (ovum) and ends with the fusion of their pronuclei (the haploid nuclei of the sperm and ovum) and the mingling of their chromosomes to form a new cell. This fertilized ovum, known as a zygote, is a large diploid cell that is the beginning, or primordium, of a human being."[Moore, Keith L. Essentials of Human Embryology. Toronto: B.C. Decker Inc, 1988, p.2]

"Embryo: An organism in the earliest stage of development; in a man, from the time of conception to the end of the second month in the uterus."[Dox, Ida G. et al. The Harper Collins Illustrated Medical Dictionary. New York: Harper Perennial, 1993, p. 146]

"The development of a human being begins with fertilization, a process by which two highly specialized cells, the spermatozoon from the male and the oocyte from the female, unite to give rise to a new organism, the zygote." [Langman, Jan. Medical Embryology. 3rd edition. Baltimore: Williams and Wilkins, 1975, p. 3]

There are countless sources from scientists and biologists that confirm this fact because it's common knowledge. It's basic biology.

Furthermore, the hypocrisy of this argument shocks me. You want to tell me that a "clump of cells" on another planet is considered "life," but not a baby in the womb? Even scientific arguments for evolution claim that life began with a clump of cells that eventually evolved into one creature and another until it became human.

Even in our lives, we see acknowledgement of this in certain situations. In the hospital, a mother and baby are treated as two different patients. If a pregnant woman is killed, it's considered a double homicide.

I also want to point out that babies are growing in the womb. Yes, they're not independent, but neither are newborns, infants, one-year-olds, or toddlers. We all started off that way—as a baby in the womb and grew into who we are today.

Saying that because a baby is not an independent or self-determined being it gives us a right to abort the child is a flawed argument because infants, toddlers, and even children aren't independent.

What about coma patients? Some may one day wake, but some are completely brain dead and not all of them or their families wish to pull the plug on their lives. Then, you also have elderly people and people with disabilities who are totally dependent on others to help and care for them.

With this argument's logic, you can justify killing elderly, disabled, toddlers—anyone who is dependent but that's wrong.

Just because someone is dependent on another person for care—even 100 percent dependent—doesn't mean they should be killed.

<u>Argument 4</u>

The fourth argument for abortion is the claim that because a "fetus" isn't alive and is just a "clump of cells," then "it" can't feel pain. A review done by Britain's Royal College of Obstetricians and Gynaecologists said that they don't believe that the cortex is what's necessary to be able to feel pain and since a baby's cortex isn't developed until week 26, they think that a baby can't feel pain until that time.

The first problem with this argument is that abortions are still done after 26 weeks, so that information alone is false. There have even been abortions and people who want abortions to be allowed all the way up until birth.

The other problem is that pain is a subjective thing. It can't really be studied because everyone feels pain differently and individually. So, all that can be done is speculate and study.

Let me give you an analogy. Say for example that someone was walking down the street and this person had a disability—something was wrong with their brain development and they couldn't feel pain (this is a real condition that can sometimes happen, called congenital insensitivity to pain). Does that make it okay to go up and kill this person, just because they can't feel pain?

No. Absolutely not.

Even if a baby can't feel pain prior to 26 weeks of pregnancy, that doesn't change the fact that you are still murdering a human being. They have a heartbeat at 3 weeks. Their pain receptors start to develop along with their nerves at 4 weeks. At 6 weeks, they respond to touch. At 8 weeks, their cerebral cortex is formed and will have the same number of nerves that an adult has. Then, at 10 weeks, if a baby is touched, their eyes will open and close—they respond to touch.

At 12, even light stimulation of the skin gets a response out of the baby.

Keep in mind that 2 abortion procedures are done at this point—one where they use a powerful vacuum to suck the baby out and one where they rip the baby apart—literally.

At 20 weeks, a baby has all the cells in their brain that an adult has, able to fully receive pain signals—enough so that their electrical activity can be recorded by basic electroencephalography.

So, two of the most common types of abortion—and the two most horrific—are done *after* a baby can feel pain.

<u>Argument 5</u>

The fifth argument for abortion is that when abortion is legal, less maternal injury and death happens as a result of illegal abortions.

This is often an argument you see for abortion and occasionally for other things. Remember Prohibition in the 1920s? It didn't work, and people still drank illegally. The problem is when something is illegal and it's done anyway, that still doesn't justify doing something that is morally wrong. Murder is illegal and it happens all the time all around the world—thousands of people are still murdered.

When someone wants to do something wrong, they'll do it anyway, regardless of whether it's legal or not. Thus, the argument is why not go ahead and make it legal? At least, when it comes to abortion.

So, should we make murder legal? Should we make anything that's morally wrong legal just because people still do it when it's illegal?

Another aspect of this argument is that it's also hypocritical—if someone uses this argument and then believes that guns should be outlawed or harder for citizens to buy and arm themselves, then that same logic has to be applied to both abortions and gun laws. If gun were outlawed, the bad people who really want to use them will still use them. The problem then is that regular citizens won't have them to protect themselves. It's the exact same argument.

The other side of this, too, is that women will get hurt by having illegal abortions—again, I could use murder, or the gun argument. People get hurt whether it's legal or illegal, but that doesn't mean we should make murder legal, even though people still get hurt because people still commit murder, even at the risk of being arrested for it.

Just because you can make something legal doesn't mean you should.

<u>Argument 6</u>

Argument six is that the risk of a woman dying from having an abortion is significantly less than the risk of dying while giving labor.

This argument doesn't make sense at all. The risk of dying from a drug overdose is actually less than the risk of dying from a heart attack but that doesn't mean we should do it.

According to the CDC, about 700 women in labor die each year in the United States.

Yet according to the CDC, 250,000 people die from malpractice and mistakes in the medical field each year in the United States.

Does that mean we should stop seeing the doctor and hospitals? Or even worse, kill them?

Absolutely not!

Every death that happens is terrible, whether it's cancer, labor, malpractice, or abortion. But one doesn't justify the other.

<u>Argument 7</u>

The seventh argument for abortion is that women who are able to have an abortion don't have as many mental health issues as women who are denied abortions. This argument uses a study that took place where 1,000 women were polled from various states throughout the country.

The main issue with this particular study is that the women were polled 11 times after their abortions up to 6 months later.

6 months is not enough time for any guilt or regret to settle in.

The people behind this study has even admitted that it was a limited study because few women decided to sign up for it. What's worse is that a study like this is an insult to women across the country who have lived with guilt and shame after having an abortion. Abortion regret is real and the woman who suffer from it often turn to drugs and suicide. Many times, women who regret abortion haven't begun to heal until years afterward—even as much as decades later. Sometimes, they don't even realize that self-destructive behaviors they had were because of abortions they got when they were younger.

Many women have spoken out about regretting their abortions, but their stories and voices have been silenced by the mainstream media, because their stories go against the politically correct narrative and lie that tries to claim that abortion regret isn't real.

It is. One study done in 2018 links abortion to higher rates of depression, anxiety, sleep disorders, substance abuse, and other traumatic experiences.

Another study in 2017 polled 987 women and 67% of them said that they visited a psychiatrist, psychologist or counsellor after their abortion and saw increases in proscription usage for mental health issues after their abortions.

The problem is that real women who suffer from mental and emotional problems after having an abortion done are silenced and often times struggle to get their voices and stories to be heard.

<u>Argument 8</u>

The eighth argument for abortion is that it gives pregnant woman an option to kill a child in the womb who has severe disorders in the womb. This argument even goes as far as to say that in some cases where the baby will have Down syndrome, parents may not be able to financially provide or care for a disabled child.

This argument is sick and twisted. People are born with disabilities each and every day and they live with them. Simple research can show you just how amazing it is when someone with a disability lives with it and becomes stronger and overcomes obstacles in their way. And I'm not even talking about basic disabilities. Some people are born with significant abnormalities in their bodies—one true life story was about a man who was born bent over himself and lived most of his life that way. Later on, he was able to go through dozens of surgeries to have the issue corrected, but this man's strength and endurance is inspiring.

As is the strength and endurance of all people who live with disabilities every day. Suggesting that we should kill children with disabilities is absolutely disgusting and monstrous.

<u>Argument 9</u>

The ninth argument states that women who are denied abortion are more likely to become unemployed and be below the poverty line. Another argument that's used which I am combining with this one is that getting an abortion helps women not have financial issues.

The exact opposite is true. Women who get abortions often struggle to get the money to pay the bill. What most people don't know, or maybe don't research enough to know, is that abortions are expensive. Often times, women who get abortions choose to wait until later in the pregnancy to give them time to get the funds to have an abortion done.

The other aspect to this is to think about this one simple fact: abortion is a money-making business. Think about how much money abortion clinics and anyone associated with them make off women getting abortions. They don't want abortion to go away or for women to stop getting them because women are their source of making tons of money!

What's worse is that generally speaking, abortion more often happens to women of low poverty—so countless women struggle to even pay for it.

The other half of this argument points out that children are expensive to care for. But that does not justify murder—should we go around killing everyone who is poor? Absolutely not.

<u>Argument 10</u>

The tenth argument for abortion says that abortion prevents babies from being born into a world that doesn't want them. I've talked about this earlier, but this argument still doesn't justify murdering a child. Abuse and financial hardships are terrible—it's horrible for the victims and people living in these conditions. Should we go around killing all the poor people or anyone who is a victim of domestic abuse? Absolutely not.

Here's the main thing to become aware of and learn: life is hard. It will be made up of struggles and hardships. Killing a baby isn't a solution—yes, of course, you're sparing it from things that the child may suffer through in the future, but you're killing it! Killing is worse than abuse and hardship.

We all have struggles. Countless people who have gone through abuse have survived and become stronger because of it. They've gone on to share their stories and help others. Likewise, many poor people have worked hard and overcome their financial hardships.

Then, there's one final aspect against this argument: you can't predict the future. How do you know what kind of hardships that child will endure? Not every child aborted will go on to have severe financial and/or physical abuse.

You're killing a human being—a human with a future who will one day have goals, likes, dislikes, hobbies, and a future job and passion—that life is not yours to take.

<u>Argument 11</u>

With this argument, I'm once again combining it with another. This argument justifies abortion by saying it reduces welfare costs because a lot of women who have abortions are poor and don't have financial stability, so their children, if born, will likely need financial assistance.

The other half of this argument says that abortion reduces crime because some women who have abortions may give birth to criminals.

To the first half, I'll repeat my previous case—just because a child is born poor does not justify killing him or her. Yes, when people need financial assistance, it increases the cost of welfare to taxpayers. So, should we go around killing everyone on welfare?

This country needs better methods of offering financial help. The entire country, in fact, is in an economic crisis and countless people are having difficulties and hardship right now. That means that we should work to fix that problem—not end a life that may or may not end up poor—and may or may not later on overcome that and come to do great things with his or her life.

To the second half of this argument, that some women may give birth to criminals, this is a deep one. You could ask the question: if you could time travel and kill Hitler in the womb before he was born, would you? The answer to that, I'm sure, has many different answers, but the main conclusion is this: when you start to argue and say things like this, then you're trying to play God.

Humans have no right to be God. He decides who lives and who goes on to eternity. He alone sees the future and knows what will happen. Even if you don't believe in God, I'm sure you understand that humans can't see the future and, therefore, it's not up to us to decide who gets to live or die before they're even born—and before we know what they'll go on to do and become.

Here is something to think on for a while: when you kill a baby, you never know what they'll grow up to do—or who they'll grow up to be.

In the same way that some women who have abortions will give birth to a criminal, some women who have abortions will give birth to a hero.

<u>Argument 12</u>

The twelfth argument is one that I can't even believe some people think is a decent justification for abortion, but it is, so here we are. Abortion is a means of population control.

Even if you thought that this was a morally correct thing to think—which, it's not—what most people don't realize is that there has actually been a severe decline in fertility rates around the world. And in Japan, Spain, and similar countries, their population will be halved in the next century.

The reasons for this are twofold—less people are having children all around the world, and more women are having abortions. All of this results in less children being born, and thus, the population is not increasing like you'd think—and certainly doesn't need to be controlled. Some countries, like China, will see a bigger population crisis in the future as the older generations die out. Younger generations who aren't getting married or aren't having children will soon grow older and then, there won't be enough children to keep up finances in the work force.

Yet, even if this wasn't the case, as previously mentioned, we humans have no right to play God and try to control the population by murdering innocent people.

What the Bible Says About Abortion

What does God and the Bible say about abortion?

Exodus 20:13 – *"Thou shalt not kill."*

The most obvious one is not to kill—murder is so wrong in God's eyes that 1 John 3:15 says, *"Whosoever hateth his brother is a murderer: and ye know that no murderer hath eternal life abiding in him."* In God's eyes, even hating someone is the same as committing murder—that's how holy and pure God is.

Isaiah 49:1 – *"Listen, O isles, unto me; and hearken, ye people, from far; The LORD hath called me from the womb; from the bowels of my mother hath he made mention of my name."*

This isn't the first verse in the Bible that talks about how God knows us in our mother's womb. But the main reason why abortion is wrong is that it's robbing someone of life—life that God already knows and values, and has a name and a plan for, even before the baby is conceived inside his or her mother's womb.

Exodus 21:22 *"If men strive, and hurt a woman with child, so that her fruit depart from her, and yet no mischief follow: he shall be surely punished, according as the woman's husband will lay upon him; and he shall pay as the judges determine."*

This is in the Old Testament Law; strict punishments for anyone who murders a pregnant woman and her baby.

Jeremiah 1:5 – "*Before I formed thee in the belly I knew thee; and before thou camest forth out of the womb I sanctified thee, and I ordained thee a prophet unto the nations.*"

Here, God is speaking directly to the prophet, Jeremiah, but the important thing to see here is that God already knew Jeremiah in the womb and knew that He would one day become a prophet to speak to the nations in God's name. Yes, God knows every baby that is going to be aborted, but even though He knows that baby is going to be aborted, we have no right to kill that child.

Luke 1:41 – "*And it came to pass, that, when Elisabeth heard the salutation of Mary, the babe leaped in her womb; and Elisabeth was filled with the Holy Ghost.*"

The babe leaped in Elizabeth's womb at the sound of Mary's voice—babies can hear in the womb and they can move and react and do summersaults and so many amazing things; they are humans and we have no more right to take their life than we do an innocent person walking out on the streets.

Proverbs 6:16-19 – "*These six things doth the LORD hate: yea, seven are an abomination unto him: A proud look, a lying tongue, and hands that shed innocent blood, a heart that deviseth wicked imaginations, feet that be swift in running to mischief, a false witness that speaketh lies, and he that soweth discord among brethren.*"

God hates when innocent blood is shed. He doesn't simply dislike it; He hates it—because He is good and holy and shedding innocent blood is evil.

Ecclesiastes 11:5 – *"As thou knowest not what is the way of the spirit, nor how the bones do grow in the womb of her that is with child: even so thou knowest not the works of God who maketh all."*

God creates every human being. He forms us in our mother's wombs and knows every intricacy of how a human body is formed. We only barely grasp how human bodies are formed but we have no idea how life was created. There are many mysteries that we as humans can't understand, don't have answers to, and can't explain because the mysteries and complexities of God are far too great for our minds to comprehend.

All life is precious. All life comes from God. He is sovereign and in control and, therefore, only He has the right to know when a life will move from this life and into eternity.

Psalm 106: 38 *"And shed innocent blood, even the blood of their sons and of their daughters, whom they sacrificed unto the idols of Canaan: and the land was polluted with blood."*

This goes back to the Canaanites and other cultures who sacrificed their children to idols. Abortion is no different—it's just done to idols of greed and money, of education and opportunities, than to stone idols.

And these last two verses go together:

Psalms 22:10 – *"I was cast upon thee from the womb: thou art my God from my mother's belly."*

Psalms 139: 1-17

LIFE: LIFE IS FOR EVERYONE

"O lord, thou hast searched me, and known me. Thou knowest my downsitting and mine uprising, thou understandest my thought afar off. Thou compassest my path and my lying down, and art acquainted with all my ways. For there is not a word in my tongue, but, lo, O Lord, thou knowest it altogether. Thou hast beset me behind and before, and laid thine hand upon me. Such knowledge is too wonderful for me; it is high, I cannot attain unto it. Whither shall I go from thy spirit? or whither shall I flee from thy presence? If I ascend up into heaven, thou art there: if I make my bed in hell, behold, thou art there. If I take the wings of the morning, and dwell in the uttermost parts of the sea; even there shall thy hand lead me, and thy right hand shall hold me. If I say, Surely the darkness shall cover me; even the night shall be light about me. Yea, the darkness hideth not from thee; but the night shineth as the day: the darkness and the light are both alike to thee. For thou hast possessed my reins: thou hast covered me in my mother's womb. I will praise thee; for I am fearfully and wonderfully made: marvelous are thy works; and that my soul knoweth right well. My substance was not hid from thee, when I was made in secret, and curiously wrought in the lowest parts of the earth. Thine eyes did see my substance, yet being unperfect; and in thy book all my members were written, which in continuance were fashioned, when as yet there was none of them. How precious also are thy thoughts unto me, O God! how great is the sum of them!"

Can you imagine, just for one moment, as God forms you in your mother's womb. He thinks of you, knows your name, your hair color, your eye color, what you will like and dislike, the things you'll grow up to accomplish, the children you may have, the job you'll have, who you'll marry or if you'll marry, every moment you laugh and all the tears that you cry—God knows it all.

And even before you were conceived, God chose to come to earth as Jesus Christ and die on the cross for your sins. He saw that your life was worth saving!

So, why do we not see that all lives are worth saving, that babies lives are worth saving?

"For thou hast possessed my reins: thou hast covered me in my mother's womb. I will praise thee; for I am fearfully and wonderfully made: marvelous are thy works; and that my soul knoweth right well."

A Final Note

I f you have gotten an abortion, do not feel as if you are beyond forgiveness or saving. Post-abortion guilt is extremely real—both for surviving children whose siblings were aborted, to mothers who got abortions at one time in their life, and even to fathers who either pushed for their child to be aborted, went along with it, or who lost their children to abortion behind their back.

God died for all our sins—whether it's abortion, or any number of sins that we commit because we live in a sin fallen world. You are worth being saved. You faced a great loss and that loss is very real to you. We all make mistakes, but God knew your choice before you made it. God is standing with His arms open wide, ready and waiting for you to accept Him and the forgiveness and love that He freely offers.

Just like the parable Jesus told of the prodigal son. The son demanded that his father give him his inheritance, so he did. But what did the son do? He went and squandered it and ended up feeding from the same food that pigs eat. He realized how low he had fallen and that even his father's servants eat better than these pigs. So, he ran home and prepared to beg his father to at least make him a servant, but his father ran to him and embraced him. He was so excited that his son came home that he threw a feast and celebrated! That's the same that God does for us.

Jesus came to earth and lived a perfect, sinless life because He knew that we never could. He died on the cross and paid the penalty of death for our sins, as if we were bailed out of jail. He paid the debt that we owed God because we broke His holy Law. God, as the just Judge of the Universe, couldn't just let crime go unpunished. But Jesus took the punishment for us, and He rose again so that we could have everlasting life with Him.

God loves you so much, just like He loves every single child formed in their mother's womb. He knew Hitler before Hitler was formed in his mother's womb too and so many countless innocents were murdered because of Hitler. Yet, he was born, and lived, because all of us have free will—the will to choose good or to do evil. We will never be perfect because the world is fallen, but one day, God promises that He will eradicate all evil. There will be no more death or sorrow and life will once again be totally perfect, as it was always meant to be.

Make the right choice today. Remember that adoption is an option and, yes, I do believe that we need to work on our adoption system much, much more—more money and more help, and making it easier for good people to adopt kids and harder for horrible people to adopt children. I've had trouble having children of my own, and I would give anything to be able to adopt a child, but right now, we can't afford it. My heart breaks every time I see a mother with a child, and it breaks even more to see children aborted. I would take in every single aborted child if I could just save their lives. It's why I'm so passionate about the subject. And I know there are countless other women like me who would give anything to have a child of our own.

Safe a life today.

Don't miss out!

Visit the website below and you can sign up to receive emails whenever Joanna White publishes a new book. There's no charge and no obligation.

https://books2read.com/r/B-A-DNHG-HICYB

Connecting independent readers to independent writers.

Also by Joanna White

The Republic Chronicles
Light Magi
Dark Magi

The Valiant Series
Hunter
Shifter
Samurai
Assassin
Forgotten
Sightless
Rebels
Reclaimed
Healed

Standalone
What Is Love
Life: Life Is For Everyone

Watch for more at https://www.authorjoannawhite.com.

About the Author

Joanna White is a Christian Author and fangirl. Hunter and Shifter are the first two books in her debut series, called the Valiant Series. She writes Fantasy, Science Fiction, Contemporary Romance, Historical Fiction, Nonfiction, and more. Her short stories have been featured in several anthologies.

She graduated from Full Sail University with a BFA in Creative Writing For Entertainment. Ever since she was ten years old, she's been writing stories and has a deep passion for writing and creating stories, worlds, characters, and plots that readers can immerse themselves in. In 2020, she reached her personal goal of writing a million words in a year. Most of all, Joanna loves God, her family, staying at home, and being a total nerd.

To stay updated and find out more about her novels, where her inspiration comes from, games, giveaways, and more, visit her website at: authorjoannawhite.com

Read more at https://www.authorjoannawhite.com.